# KURT COBAIN

# KURT COBAIN

## Voice of a Generation

### CHRIS MOLANPHY

BARNES
&NOBLE
BOOKS

## DEDICATION

This book is dedicated to my downstairs cousins, who taught me how cool music sounds at full blast; and my friend Jay, who introduced me to "Smells Like Teen Spirit" in 1991 and blew my mind.

ISBN 0-7607-4298-7

Editors: Rosy Ngo and Lindsay Herman
Art Director: Kevin Ullrich
Designer: Kevin Baier
Photography Editor: Janice Ackerman
Photography Researcher: Christy Whitney
Production Manager: Richela Fabian Morgan

Color separations by Bright Arts Graphics (S) Pte Ltd.
Printed in Belgium by Proost.

1 3 5 7 9 10 8 6 4 2

# CONTENTS

# INTRODUCTION
# OVERBORED & SELF-ASSURED

ALTHOUGH ONE OF THE MOST REVERED AND ANALYZED ARTISTS at the end of the twentieth century, Kurt Cobain remains surprisingly difficult to understand. In life, he drifted from place to place and person to person, frustrating any attempts—even by the people he loved—to know him fully. In his brief, incandescent years of fame with Nirvana, he was the subject of apocryphal stories and half-truths, many of which he spawned himself. And in death, Cobain left music fans all over the world in awe of his talent and still yearning to know what made someone so gifted so troubled, what made such a hard-living person so perceptive and empathetic. How did Kurt Cobain speak for so many of us if he couldn't speak for himself?

Inarguably, Kurt spoke best through his music. There is a kind of clarity in his lyrics, which, at first, don't seem clear at all. And his melodies are at once bracingly innovative and instantly familiar. To be attracted to Nirvana's music is to participate in an accidental movement, a restless youth culture, and Kurt's songs reflect the passionate, contemptuous, witty people who love them. Inaugurating a decade of cultural irony and a period of social discontent, Kurt was the vehicle through which the 1990s began. The music of Nirvana marked a major generational shift in pop culture because it welcomed, perhaps inadvertently, so many people into what Kurt called, in his most famous song, "our little group." He may not have been the spokesman of his generation but he was surely the quintessence of it.

Rather than act as a spokesman, Cobain eluded simple explanation at every opportunity. He preferred to be examined through his art—his music, his lyrics, his painting and sculpture. But his art also included the way he carried himself—onstage, in photographs, on MTV—the way he looked away from fans and then, at a key moment, stared intently back. Even before he was famous, Cobain thought carefully about how he was perceived. By the time he'd become a reluctant superstar, he was constantly grappling with the media and his demigod image. To look at the photographs contained in this book is, therefore, to seek a better understanding of an artist creating himself as he went along.

**ABOVE:** An outtake from the July 1991 photo session that produced the cover of Nirvana's *Nevermind* album, this photo offers Kurt as the famous swimming baby all grown up. More than a decade later, it also captures Kurt the way the world remembers him: intense, perceptive, insular, alone.

OVERBORED & SELF-ASSURED    9

*ABOVE:* Kurt performs at a stop on the 1993 *In Utero* tour. Fans at these shows observed the dichotomy of Kurt in all of its forms: at various moments he was charming or surly, a showman or a slacker, totally committed or completely bored.

As his band mates, friends, family, and many biographers have revealed, Cobain was a mass of contradictions. He could be gentle but also destructive. Possessing natural good looks beneath his unwashed hair and ragged clothes, he carried himself with self-flagellating modesty and yet could be self-aggrandizing in the next breath. Although Cobain never completed high school, he was smart and perceptive. He could be stridently political but remained ambivalent about the world and his place in it. He came of age believing the code of punk without ever losing his love of pop—a big reason why his music was embraced by such a wide audience.

Perhaps most controversially, although Cobain professed disinterest in fame and was often a self-defeating rock star, he was privately very ambitious and consistently sought attention. The most poignant, memorable images associated with Nirvana's music—*Nevermind*'s dollar-chasing baby, the anarchy cheerleaders of "Smells Like Teen Spirit," the onstage destruction of instruments—were ideas concocted by Kurt.

Images of Kurt Cobain are pieces of art in and of themselves. Like his songs, they are the truest artifacts we have to represent him, unspoiled by myth making—ours, the media's, or Cobain's. Yet, again like his songs, these photographs invite interpretation: we project ideas, wishes, *ourselves* onto Cobain. As he did in his brief life, he absorbs all of our own contradictions—our need to rebel and our need to belong, our desire to look cool and our wish to look away.

ABOVE: However Kurt felt about the mechanics of fame, he used them to brilliant advantage. But often, fame used him. By 1993, less than a year before the end of Kurt's life, his image had become iconic to a generation of music fans and to the culture at large.

## CHAPTER ONE

# BEEN A SON

IN THE YEARS BEFORE NIRVANA'S BREAKTHROUGH, KURT COBAIN made an art out of defying expectations. Indeed, he was often just defiant—raging against the provincial mentality he perceived around him and rebelling when his happy childhood turned into a troubled adolescence. But the obstacles he overcame were sometimes of his own making; if Cobain amounted to more than could have been expected, it's because he set such low expectations himself. The truth is that Kurt had both raw talent and a drive to succeed. The persona he came to embody later—punk purist, slacker icon—is contradicted by the facts of his youth. Everything that would one day make Nirvana great came from Cobain's duality.

Born on February 20, 1967, Kurt Donald Cobain has been called the most famous thing to come out of Aberdeen, Washington. Located on the southern edge of Washington's Olympic Peninsula, where the Wishkah and Chehalis rivers meet, and surrounded by towering forests and mountains, Aberdeen was dominated for decades by the logging industry. But the Aberdeen of the late 1960s was beset by a depressed economy and high unemployment. Kurt's father, Donald Cobain, was a twenty-one-year-old mechanic hard-pressed to pay his rent. Months earlier, Donald had married a pregnant Wendy Fradenberg, nineteen years old and a recent high school graduate.

Yet Kurt's early childhood, spent in a series of tiny houses in Aberdeen and in the adjacent town of Hoquiam, was anything but unpleasant. A cheerful, gregarious child, he was much beloved by his family, with his grandparents and aunts doting on him.

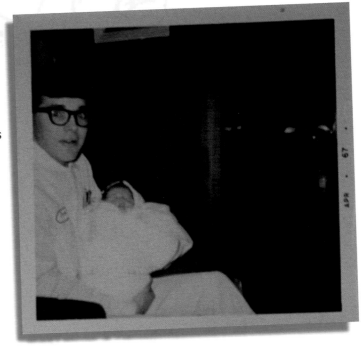

**ABOVE:** Born into a modest home in Hoquiam, Washington, Kurt Donald Cobain was the center of attention from birth. Here, he is held by his father, Donald.

ABOVE: Although much of Kurt's adolescence was spent shuffling from one relative's household to another's, Kurt found one consistent presence throughout these years: music. With a large musical family on his mother's side, Kurt loved combing through his aunts' and uncles' record collections and tagging along on his Uncle Chuck's band rehearsals and local gigs. Pictured here at a wedding reception where Chuck's band was performing, fourteen-year-old Kurt had hopped behind his uncle's drum set while the band paused for a break.

CLOCKWISE FROM TOP: Kurt showed an interest in music as a baby, singing at the top of his lungs when barely two years old.

Though he always received toys on Christmas, Kurt would sometimes find a piece of coal at the bottom of his stocking—this was done mainly as a joke but also served as a reminder for the occasionally unruly child to behave himself.

Christmas was something of a formative holiday for Kurt—visits to relatives, including his guitar-playing Aunt Mari and Uncle Chuck, encouraged his early musical interests, as he would watch family jam sessions, rapt.

Kurt was a hyperactive young boy, and his parents allowed him to burn energy by running around their backyard or playing with toys. Around the time this picture (with sister Kim) was taken, Kurt's parents gave him a set of Mickey Mouse drums, the first musical instrument he called his own and an excellent outlet for his boundless energy.

As Kurt grew, his energy manifested itself as hyperactivity, and for a few months in grade school he was treated with sedatives. By age five, Cobain was showing a facility for both music and art—he could pick out tunes on the piano and was exceptional at drawing, even before entering elementary school.

In 1976 came the event that would permanently change Kurt's demeanor—his parents' divorce. Caused by the strains of a young marriage, the split deeply affected the nine-year-old, and he began to withdraw emotionally. Wendy won custody of Kurt and his sister Kim, but within months he asked to live with his father, who had moved into a trailer with Kurt's grandparents. Though Donald Cobain assured his son they would remain close, within two years he'd remarried and bought a house in nearby Montesano with his new wife and stepchildren. Meanwhile, Kurt's mother was living with a new boyfriend—the first of several. Though neither of Kurt's parents ever fully abandoned him, he nonetheless felt betrayed.

While adolescence is usually marked by self-consciousness and a fear of alienation, as a teenager, Kurt seemed to alienate himself. At fourteen, he began making short films that depicted death, even his own. He also talked casually with school friends about murder and suicide—a frequent theme of his art. He wrote extensive journals in spiral-bound notebooks, recounting dreams and chronicling fantasies that were eloquent and impressionistic. Perhaps unsurprisingly, he started consuming alcohol, marijuana, and LSD regularly. Yet Kurt the teenager still wasn't the wholesale rejecter of social convention and suburban ambition that he would be known as later in life: he tried out for the high school football squad, threw discus for the track-and-field team, and—despite his small frame—became a varsity wrestler.

During these years, Kurt wasn't much of a nihilist or a punk when it came to music, either. His young tastes were all-encompassing, which would explain the broad appeal of the music he would write with Nirvana. As a child, Kurt loved pop songs—his favorite was Terry Jacks' 1974 light-folk ditty "Seasons in the Sun"—and he soon developed a serious interest in the Beatles. While learning the guitar at fourteen, he requested that his instructor teach him the usual teen-boy favorites, "Stairway to Heaven" and "Back in Black." His first concerts included Sammy Hagar and Judas Priest, and among

RIGHT: With his piercing blue eyes and wry smile, Kurt was photogenic practically from birth, and his magnetic personality was in evidence when he was barely out of diapers. The main difference between young Kurt and older Kurt was that he was habitually cheerful as a child, a contrast to his sullen temperament as an adolescent and adult.

his first albums was REO Speedwagon's pop-rock smash *Hi Infidelity*. But it would be reductive to call the teenage Cobain a metalhead—he appreciated quirky, experimental music, too, including eclectic new-wavers Oingo Boingo and an album his aunt had given him by the Bonzo Dog Band, a '60s musical-comedy act.

Kurt's fascination with punk was sparked at a 1983 Melvins concert in a Montesano supermarket parking lot. When punk music finally entered his life, the sixteen year old needed it not so much for musical inspiration as for spiritual freedom; he attached himself not simply to the music but also to the ethic. For Kurt, punk meant the denial of everything that came before, and it offered him a surrogate family of misfits. Musically, punk's raw sound and do-it-yourself aesthetic helped foster Kurt's creativity, but what he really took from punk was its lack of strictures and its embrace of the perverse. "Punk is freedom," Kurt would later say in interviews as a kind of mantra, but for him it was also a burden, one that compelled him to reject anything in the mainstream. The punk scene would actually serve to emphasize his contrary nature. In fact, Kurt never stopped listening to pop and metal, and he would later turn away from the asceticism of punk when its gatekeepers made him feel unwelcome. But while still in his teens, Kurt began wearing nothing but punk band T-shirts.

Kurt lived with his father and stepmother into his early teenage years, but his inability to adapt to his father's new family became unbearable. Returning to his mother's house was a short-lived solution. He finally left home, left school—he was flunking

THIS PAGE: Before his parents' divorce, Kurt was a charismatic boy with an infectious laugh and ceaseless enthusiasm—relatives found him effortlessly charming. His young interests were classic for an all-American kid: sledding down snowy Aberdeen hills, bicycling around town, and playing baseball.

everything except art class—and began to rotate from one living arrangement to the next, sometimes staying with relatives, then families of friends. Finally, he spent several months on the street.

During this itinerant period, Kurt met up with Krist Novoselic, an old schoolmate two years his senior, and they started jamming together after Kurt settled at a friend's house. Some of Kurt's own compositions made it into their jam sessions, with Novoselic's meaty bass lines underpinning Cobain's wiry melodies. With friend Aaron Burckhard on drums, Kurt and Krist formed a band in 1986. Fronted and fueled by Kurt, the trio practiced for hours each night; Kurt in particular showed no compunction in tinkering with his guitar into the wee hours, long after his friends had grown bored with jamming.

This incarnation of the then-unnamed group played its first gig at a house party in Raymond, Washington, in the winter of 1987, for a less than appreciative beer-brawl crowd. More house parties followed, each gig under a different name (including, briefly, Skid Row), and Kurt, in his perverse way, became more of a showman, wearing garish clothes and smashing instruments to get attention.

It was clear that Kurt was outgrowing Aberdeen. In the spring of 1987, Kurt and his girlfriend, Tracy Marander, packed their things and moved sixty-five miles (104.5km) to Olympia, a city not much larger than Aberdeen but with a deep-rooted college culture and a burgeoning rock scene. In more ways than one, this was the turning point for Kurt: he would rarely return to Aberdeen again; his band would soon begin its recording career, and Kurt would finally give the band a name.

*Most Improved-Jackie Zimmerman, Kevin Alexander, and Kelly McCarroll. Most Coachable-Theresa Napiontek, Most Valuable-Dianne Moore, Most Inspirational-Renee Golden. Most Improved-Bret Duvall, Most Coachable-Gary Moore, and Most Valuable-Guy Barber, and Most Inspirational HW, Guy Barker, LW Mike Campbell. Boys Track· Coach-Joel Tyndell, Managers· Tim Roberts, Leon Gross, Gary Moore, Guy Barber, Bob Denholm, Scott Sutherby, Larry Quinn, Mark Sutherby, Bryan Alexander, Phil Schilling, Cameron Torrens, Bret Duvall, Mike Peterson, Steve Baxter, Steve Brittain, Scott Osborne, Darrin Bies, Ron Davis, **Kurt Cobain**, Dan Ackley, John Herzog, Scott Cokely. Girls·Track· Coach· Cindy Davidson, Managers· Mare Peterson, Marci Hammock, M. Murphie, T. Peterson, K. McEvoy, B. Crass, V. Engh, K. Focht, D. Moore, G. Swinhart, L. Brumfield, L. Powell, N. Hutchinson, T. Ward, A. Butterfield, J. Aimmerman, K. Alexander, T. Napiontek, K. Dujmov, R. Golden, T. Brumfield, L. L. Norberg, H. McClean, A. Rottle, S. Huffman, L. Johnson, L. Henson, B. Brisco, D. Chandler, N. Gonsalves, J. Hliboki, D. Hockett, J. Kim, D. McAlpin, K. McCarroll, T. Menz, W. Shields, R S Tagman, A. Torens, L. Vessey, K. Viebrock.*

ABOVE: Not yet the malcontent he would become as a teenager, in the seventh grade, Kurt was a member of Montesano Junior High School's track team.

ABOVE: Kurt's grandfather Leland Cobain holds an album of family photos, 2003. Although this well-known Cobain family portrait from Christmas 1974 (at left) depicts a contented couple, in fact, Wendy and Donald's relationship was deteriorating, and they divorced two years later. After the divorce and Donald's remarriage, Kurt lived rather uncomfortably with his father and new stepfamily, while Kim remained with Wendy in Aberdeen. As he struggled with loyalty issues between his mother and father, Kurt was always protective of his little sister. Some eighteen years after this picture (at right) was taken, Kim came out to Kurt, and he immediately expressed concern for her safety in Aberdeen—a town not known for tolerance toward homosexuals.

LEFT: Kurt possessed exceptional artistic talent, and had an uncanny knack for drawing. Grandfather Leland Cobain once prodded six-year-old Kurt to admit that he'd been tracing cartoon characters, before observing that the boy could draw them freehand. This is one of the myriad drawings Kurt gave him and his wife, Iris.

BELOW: Iris Cobain, Kurt's grandmother, was a primary influence on his artistic inclinations. She collected crafts and was herself a hobbyist artist, teaching Kurt how to draw with toothpicks on wild mushrooms. Many of Kurt's early drawings and paintings were for her.

ABOVE: Aberdeen punk rockers the Melvins single-handedly prompted Kurt's interest in punk, with a 1983 concert in a Montesano supermarket parking lot. Guitarist Roger "Buzz" Osborne (right) became a spiritual big brother to Kurt and let the teenager work as a roadie for the band on small club tours in the late '80s. Drummer Dale Crover (center) sat in with Nirvana as they struggled to find a drummer and even appeared on their first demos with Seattle producer Jack Endino in 1988. Though the Melvins never earned much more than a cult following, Kurt loyally supported the band's career even after his own mainstream success.

OPPOSITE TOP: The now-legendary Young Street Bridge in Aberdeen, made immortal in Nirvana's song "Something in the Way," was definitely a hideaway for Kurt—where he and his friends would hang out and smoke pot, or where he'd dawdle alone after getting kicked out of a friend's house. However, most of his intimates doubt that he actually lived "underneath the bridge," as he would later claim in interviews and insinuate in lyrics.

OPPOSITE BOTTOM: The Coral Room bar and restaurant in Olympia was frequented by Kurt and his friends in the mid- to late-1980s. Kurt and Tracy Marander had moved into an Olympia studio apartment in 1987, and Kurt's young band benefited from the city's college-rock community, first playing private parties, then a local radio show, and eventually a recurring gig at Tacoma's Community World Theater.

# CHAPTER TWO

# BIG CHEESE, MAKE ME

**W**HILE THE IMAGE OF KURT COBAIN AS A PRETERNATURALLY gifted slacker remains his primary representation in pop culture, in truth, when inspired, Kurt was as driven as a bull, discovering the work ethic that seemed to elude him in other areas of life. The years of Nirvana's ascension, before the onset of global fame, were arguably the most exciting in Cobain's life. With his friend and band mate Krist Novoselic in full support, punk rock became the outlet that would fuse and define Cobain's latent talents—his artistic perceptiveness, his ear for melody, and his furious energy.

In January 1988, the still-unnamed band paid to record a demo with renowned Seattle producer Jack Endino. Kurt came armed with dozens of songs. A few weeks after the sessions, Kurt finally settled on the name Nirvana—"the attainment of perfection"—after watching a late-night television program on Buddhism. With a demo tape and a permanent band name, Kurt began contacting record labels. Endino, too, passed the tape along to his acquaintances in the fledgling Seattle music scene, and the band eventually attracted the attention of indie-rock label Sub Pop. With a single, a cover of the Shocking Blue's "Love Buzz" backed with Kurt's own "Big Cheese," released in late 1988, and a steady stream of gigs, Nirvana gradually developed a following both in their home base of Olympia and in Seattle.

While Kurt worked diligently at the band and his music, he lived modestly, shrank from responsibility, and had difficulty communicating, even with those closest to him. He had trouble holding down a job—Kurt endured various stints as a carpet layer and a janitor—but he wasn't so much rebellious as withdrawn, often leaving jobs before bosses could fire him. Before a show, Kurt liked to predict how badly it would go, only to impress the audience, his band mates, and even himself with their incendiary performances. Even relationships within the band were circumscribed by Kurt's insularity: though Nirvana went through a series of drummers before settling on its final lineup, Kurt never directly fired any of them because he feared confrontation. (Usually, a drummer would only know he was out if Kurt stopped talking to him.) As openly as

*ABOVE:* Nirvana played Seattle's HUB Ballroom in February 1989. Though they were more earnest performers at this time, there are early signs of Kurt's ironic sense of humor here—note the band's poster of Elvis Presley, doctored to make him look like glam-metal star Alice Cooper; and Kurt's Texas T-shirt, complete with Lone Star, a symbol of mainstream, conservative culture.

ABOVE: The "grunge" imagery that would become mainstream after Nirvana's breakthrough was already part of Kurt's look by 1990.

LEFT: Tall, gregarious, and easygoing, Croatian-American Krist Novoselic (left) would remain the constant in Cobain's life. Together they moved to Olympia and established themselves in the city's college-oriented, band-friendly scene. Here, Kurt wears one of the many T-shirts in his collection celebrating then-obscure punk bands. Scratch Acid, a Texas-based band, later spawned '90s noise rockers the Jesus Lizard.

he expressed himself in his art, Cobain would censor himself around people, unwilling to build expectations he couldn't fulfill.

The person who most endured Kurt's introversion was his first girlfriend, Tracy Marander. They shared an apartment in Olympia with a menagerie of pets—they'd bonded, in part, over a love of animals. Marander's contribution to early Nirvana can hardly be overstated. In addition to providing both financial and emotional support for Kurt, she and Krist's girlfriend, Shelli, acted as de facto managers and bookers for the band. Tracy even got Nirvana one of its best—and steadiest—early gigs, at Tacoma's Community World Theater, by passing a tape of a radio appearance to the theater owner. But while Kurt loved Tracy and deeply appreciated her support, in their three years together he kept her at a distance, often communicating with her through notes. Tracy's attempts to confront him about commitment would only push him further away. Though he remained faithful through most of their relationship, Tracy—ironically, Kurt's longest-lasting girlfriend—never completely pierced Kurt's emotional armor.

The most direct way Kurt communicated was through songs, and though his lyrics were circuitous and oblique, they expressed a clear emotional truth. Frustrated with his impeded communication with Tracy, he wrote the simple, hook-driven "About a Girl." In a few conversational verses, Cobain articulated the variety of emotions stirred during the deterioration of a relationship—sorrow, contempt, loneliness, affection. "Negative Creep," written in a fit of self-hatred and ironic wit, serves as Kurt's own autobiography and exemplifies his very un-rock star mentality in two spare, furious verses. Both early songs reflect a highly personal aspect of Cobain's lyricism, while in songs like "Floyd the Barber,"—a gruesome parody of *The Andy Griffith Show*—and "Mr. Mustache"—a first-person testimonial of a meat-eating macho man—he created scenarios and narrators through which he could shrewdly convey his perspective. These songs appeared on *Bleach*, Nirvana's June 1989 debut album, which encapsulated Kurt Cobain's life in microcosm: passionate but indirect, ostensibly punk but innately populist, underestimated but ultimately admired.

Recorded for Sub Pop with producer Endino and drummer Chad Channing, *Bleach* was not an instant success but rather a slow burn, amassing steady sales into 1990 despite Sub Pop's limited promotional resources. Critics weren't uniformly impressed, and punk classicists sniffed at the band's thick metal overtones so reminiscent of Black Sabbath. Yet *Bleach*—with its bludgeoning sound, punk economy, and insinuating hooks—gradually won fans on college radio, spreading nationwide and crossing into Europe, where U.K. journalists were discovering the emerging Seattle scene sooner than their U.S. counterparts. In short, rather than Kurt having to foist himself upon the world, the world was coming to Kurt, much to the surprise of Washington scenesters and Cobain himself.

Having never left the Pacific Northwest, Cobain finally saw more of the world in 1989 and 1990, as Nirvana visited Europe on a bill with Seattle band Tad and toured the United States in a beat-up van. Each

Dear long lost grandparents,
  I miss you very much, which is no
excuse for my not visiting.
  I'm very busy living in Olympia
when I'm not on tour with my band.
  We've put out a single just recently
And it has sold out Already.  We are
Recording for our debut LP this monday
which will be released in March.
  In february we Are going on tour Again
to California, then we'll be back
in April only to take A break, then on the
Road Again.  I'm happier than I ever
have been.  It would be nice to hear
from you as well.      Merry Christmas
    love kurt    352-0992

Wishing you
the special happiness
of this beautiful
season.

ABOVE: Immensely proud of his budding recording career, Kurt wrote to grandparents Leland and Iris Cobain at Christmas 1988 to update them on his life in Olympia.

LEFT: Instrumental to the development of the Northwest rock scene, Sub Pop heads Bruce Pavitt and Jonathan Poneman were better marketers than they were business-men. They promoted bands with attention-getting but expensive stunts, like flying British journalists to Seattle to cover a showcase. In the late '80s, Sub Pop signed the trini-ty of quintessential grunge bands: Soundgarden, Mudhoney, and Nirvana.

city found more fans familiar with *Bleach* and anticipating Nirvana's arrival. By the fall of 1990, Nirvana was opening for veteran noise rockers Sonic Youth. Following the indie legends' tour bus in their own cramped van, Nirvana felt like their little-brother band, and Kurt innately trusted the musicians, who had grown in celebrity since their early '80s debut without compromising their sound. For their part, the members of Sonic Youth took the young band under their wing: on the recommendation of Thurston Moore and Kim Gordon, Nirvana signed with the band's management company and, later, an offshoot of its label, Geffen. But while Kurt was honored to tour with his heroes, the concert schedule was grueling, and chronic stomach problems that had plagued him since his teenage years flared up on the road. For Kurt, each stage in the band's emergence was fueled by determination but suffused with mixed emotions.

This mix of drive and pain brought Nirvana to the threshold of fame. Having grown frustrated with the band's succession of drummers, Cobain in late 1990 finally found a worthy timekeeper in Dave Grohl, formerly of Washington, D.C., bands Scream and Dain Bramage. Equally dissatisfied with Sub Pop's limited resources, Cobain hired managers to find the band a major-label deal, ultimately signing with David Geffen's DGC Records in early 1991. Meanwhile, a short-lived passionate relationship with a new girlfriend in 1990

ABOVE: Chad Channing (left) wasn't Nirvana's first drummer nor even the first to be recorded, but he was present on *Bleach* and through much of the band's period on Sub Pop Records. Of the series of drummers who played with Kurt and Krist before the joining of Dave Grohl in 1990, Channing lasted the longest—just under two years.

gave Kurt plenty of songwriting fodder for Nirvana's next album. For Kurt and for Nirvana, everything was about to change.

Kurt underwent a personal transformation as he entrenched himself in the Washington rock scene, which at the turn of the 1990s was immersed in ardent liberal politics. Though Kurt had always felt alienated by male aggression in his logging hometown and was repelled by yuppie ambition in general, he had until then been fairly apolitical. In Olympia, his new friends formally introduced him to feminist ideals and progressive politics, which in that city's youth culture went hand in hand with punk agitprop. Among his new friends were Tobi Vail and Kathleen Hanna, who would later form Bikini Kill, a band that melded strident punk with vehement feminism and spawned the riot grrrl movement. Kurt dated Tobi in the summer of 1990, and he was enraptured both with her and with the polemical rock scene that emerged around her band. But Vail never took her relationship with Kurt as seriously as he did, and she broke it off six months after it began. Their short affair mirrored Kurt's tense relationship with the Northwest rock scene—he felt eternally inadequate around its hard-core, pop-rejecting punks. For Tobi, the fling with Kurt may have been a distraction, but for Kurt the transformation was permanent. As Nirvana grew famous, he and Krist became more outwardly political, supporting numerous liberal causes, and Kurt would come to be remembered as one of rock's most unabashedly feminist male musicians.

Reeling from his abrupt breakup with Vail and fired by his broadening social awareness, Kurt spent late 1990 and early 1991 writing some of his most profound songs. Nirvana recorded their second album, *Nevermind*, with producer Butch Vig in the spring of 1991. Musically, Kurt's new songs encompassed the breadth of his loves, fusing the directness of punk with pop melodies. Lyrically, several of them—especially "Drain You" and "Lounge Act"—touched on the still-fresh breakup with Vail, but because of his impressionistic writing style, Kurt's songs took on broader meanings.

Perhaps the strongest song, however, was so oblique that it became something of an anthem for a worldwide population of young music fans. Teen Spirit was a brand of deodorant that Vail, in a bit of ironic humor, liked to wear; fellow Bikini Kill member Hanna once teased Kurt by writing on a wall "Kurt smells like Teen Spirit," implying that Vail's scent was on him. Starting as an in-joke and private rant, the song "Smells Like Teen Spirit" took on a life of its own. Kurt redrafted the lyrics repeatedly, and as they evolved they encapsulated his fury, ambivalence, boredom, defiance, and rejection. Musically, the song created the blueprint for both Nirvana's music and much of the next decade of modern rock: muted, sinister verses paired with exploding choruses. Cobain, Novoselic, and Grohl joked about their "Pixies rip-off," worrying that the quiet-loud "Smells Like Teen Spirit" was too obviously derivative of the '80s indie-rock band; Kurt even admitted to adapting the guitar riff from Boston's old schlock-rock hit "More Than a Feeling." But the pastiche overcame Kurt's influences, fusing them into something new.

**ABOVE AND INSET:** Bikini Kill combined impassioned feminism and a raw punk sound. In the process, the band launched the riot grrrl movement and presaged the stronger female-rocker archetype that would sweep through music in the 1990s. The performance above features drummer Tobi Vail taking a rare lead vocal turn. Vail (also inset) became Kurt's girlfriend in the summer of 1990. Bikini Kill's politics had a huge influence on Kurt, who became a committed feminist largely under the tutelage of Vail and lead singer/guitarist Kathleen Hanna. Vail's abrupt breakup with Kurt in November 1990 inspired most of the standout songs he wrote for Nirvana's *Nevermind*.

**LEFT:** A neighbor and friend of Kurt's, Slim Moon was a central figure in the Olympia rock scene. He cofounded the drone-rock band Earth with Dylan Carlson, another of Kurt's friends. Later, Moon founded the independent label Kill Rock Stars. In 1990, Moon helped Kurt acclimate to Olympia and observed as Kurt transferred his affections from hometown girlfriend Tracy Marander to Vail.

This, finally, is how Kurt's music became the embodiment of his era: by depicting primal emotions in postmodern code. No one, least of all Kurt, could have known in 1991 that this would be the way an entire generation would want to express itself. He was just reflecting his own desire for meaning in a dead-end environment, expressing his disdain for the sell-out baby boomers who'd exchanged their once-impassioned idealism for a corporate-sponsored version of the American dream. Unbeknownst to Kurt, however, his peers shared his frustration deeply. The baby boom generation had dominated popular discourse for some three decades, with a hangover of *Big Chill* self-absorption still afflicting the culture as the 1990s began. A shadow group—one disaffected by a country deep in recession—was ready to emerge.

That Nirvana exploded from this confluence of events can be attributed—in large part—to timing. To be sure, the group benefited from circumstance no less than the Beatles did, reaching the public consciousness at an opportune moment. Like the Beatles, Nirvana came armed with indelible songs, universal messages, and years of toil. The difference was that this time the burden of zeitgeist dominance would be borne not by four men but, disproportionately, one. As the principal songwriter, sole lyricist, and strikingly visual front man of Nirvana, Kurt Cobain would be the primary vehicle of a cultural renaissance. On tour again with Sonic Youth in the summer of 1991, Kurt hadn't yet realized what an enormous burden that would be.

*LEFT:* In 1988, Jonathan Poneman (right) booked Nirvana at the bottom of his label's "Sub Pop Sunday" showcases at the Vogue in Seattle before finally agreeing to sign the band. Kurt later came to mistrust Poneman and his partner, Bruce Pavitt, and made plans to relocate to a bigger label almost immediately after Sub Pop released Nirvana's first record.

ABOVE: On the eve of *Bleach*'s release and on the brink of a breakthrough, Kurt was more focused and determined than he'd been at any other time in his life.

*OPPOSITE:* Though he avoided the flashy metal solos that were de rigueur in the late 1980s, Kurt was a well-regarded and fierce guitar player. Years later, when Nirvana became famous, even metal demigod Eddie Van Halen wanted to jam with the band onstage.

*ABOVE:* Sub Pop Records hired Alice Wheeler—a local photographer, an Aberdeen fixture, and a friend of the band—to take promotional photos for the release of *Bleach*.

*LEFT:* By 1989, the Seattle scene had already become a rock hotbed. Note the Soundgarden sticker on Kurt's guitar. Like Nirvana, the heavy rock band fronted by Chris Cornell and Kim Thayil launched its recording career on Sub Pop— Soundgarden released their first EPs two years before Nirvana released *Bleach*.

Though their earliest gigs were wobbly and played before tiny crowds, by 1989 Nirvana had established a reputation as a ferocious live act, with Kurt the clear onstage focal point.

*OPPOSITE:* Publicity shots from Nirvana's brief period as a foursome. Clockwise from top left: Kurt, drummer Chad Channing, guitarist Jason Everman (whose tenure lasted less than six months), and Krist Novoselic.

*LEFT:* One of the biggest early groups on Sub Pop, Seattle's Tad was fronted by Tad Doyle, a 300-pound (136kg) Idahoan and the band's namesake. Kurt was particularly fascinated by Doyle, whose gastrointestinal problems rivaled his own.

*BELOW:* The European tour in 1989 brought the members of Nirvana and Tad closer, with the two bands sharing the close quarters of a single van. To the U.K. press, Tad was even more representative of the grunge archetype than Nirvana— grizzled, bleak, sludgy. Though well loved in Washington, Tad was the last of the early Sub Pop bands to sign with a major label, one year before Kurt's death.

OPPOSITE: Nirvana performs at Seattle's HUB Ballroom in 1989. For Kurt, the band's live performances served as both an opportunity for spectacle and a platform for his own introspection. Though he knew how to rile up a crowd, he often internalized his performances—the unpredictable front man would either keep between-song patter to a minimum or just be inscrutable to his audience and band mates.

ABOVE: Carefree moments in Olympia, like this one in 1990, were some of the happiest for Kurt, when Nirvana's up-and-coming buzz was exciting but not yet overwhelming.

*   Nirvana   *

LOVE BUZZ
Big Cheese

Kurdt Kobain

Chris Novoselic

Chad Channing

Recorded at Reciprocal Studios
Seattle Produced by Jack Endino
Nirvana

ABOVE: This photo appeared on the back of the jacket for the *Bleach* album. Kurt's onstage destruction of instruments began early in Nirvana's career and eventually became a fairly regular part of their shows. Krist and other band mates would join in, but Kurt was the most zealous demolisher.

LEFT: Kurt gave his grandparents a slip of paper on which he scrawled the contents of Nirvana's first single on Sub Pop. Note that he was already signing the name "Kurdt," which he fancied as his rock alter ego.

ABOVE: Stage diving and crowd surfing predated the Northwest rock scene, but the grunge movement brought audience participation to new levels. Mosh pits became a rock concert staple, and attendees began fighting their way to the stage. Kurt himself was famous for diving into the audience, as evidenced during this November 12, 1991 performance in Frankfurt, Germany (bottom).

ABOVE: Replacing broken instruments was a serious expense for a fledgling band like Nirvana in the years before their breakthrough. After destroying his guitar during a show on their 1989 tour through Massachusetts, Kurt was stuck performing empty-handed at Jamaica Plain's Green Street Station. He eventually decided to reassemble a broken guitar he'd spotted hanging on a friend's wall and continued the tour with the newly mended instrument.

OPPOSITE TOP: Dan Peters of Mudhoney (left) briefly drummed with Nirvana just before permanent drummer Dave Grohl finally joined the group.

OPPOSITE BOTTOM: By the time the tour with Sonic Youth reached Washington in September 1990, Nirvana was often more anticipated than the headlining band. It was on this leg of the tour that future drummer Dave Grohl saw them perform, having been flown to Seattle at Kurt's request.

Alice Wheeler's well-known double-exposure
photo of Kurt effectively encapsulates his
ambivalence about the onset of fame: he was
simultaneously hungry for and repulsed by it.
Even as he grew wary of Nirvana's growing
audience, his fans came to appreciate his wariness—a cynicism and suspicion they shared.

ABOVE: This famous shot by British photographer Ian Tilton, taken moments after a Seattle concert in 1990, captures Kurt's vulnerability and also depicts the raw angst and mixed emotions of the entire Seattle scene. Tilton recalled that Kurt, after destroying his instruments in the frenzied show, came offstage, fell to the floor, and broke down crying. A minute later, he was fine.

OPPOSITE: By fall 1991, Kurt was on the verge of a breakthrough in more ways than one. While Nirvana toured Europe in November, their first major-label release was busy conquering mainstream American airwaves and winning over even the most rigid of punk aficionados. Kurt himself was busy courting a new girlfriend.

# CHAPTER THREE
# ENTERTAIN US

**K**URT COBAIN SPENT THE BETTER PART OF A DECADE SEEKING an audience for his music, but for him, anticipation was more exciting than execution, the vision more fulfilling than the reality. When his band finally broke through, he was utterly unprepared for the magnitude of its reception. Within four months of its release, Nirvana's *Nevermind* topped the U.S. charts, knocking 1980s superstar Michael Jackson from the number one slot. Rarely do the charts so accurately reflect, in a single week, a wholesale shift in popular culture—this was one time the numbers told a story borne out by public sentiment. Just as the social concept of "the sixties" doesn't really begin until 1963's one-two punch of Kennedy's assassination and the Beatles' breakthrough, and the concept of "the eighties" doesn't really begin until the December 1980 assassination of John Lennon, Nirvana's late-1991 breakthrough kicks off "the nineties" as we now remember them. In music, the change was swift: bands previously considered too left-of-center for mainstream tastes were brought—sometimes dragged—to center stage. Some of Cobain's indie-rock heroes—the Meat Puppets, the Butthole Surfers, the Pixies, and the Breeders—would score gold records before the alternative movement was over. Likewise, many of Cobain's Washington State contemporaries, even bands he hated, would sell as well as or better than Nirvana, riding the band's coattails. As Cobain's generation finally (almost reluctantly) took control of the culture, all of Kurt's own reclusive instincts—a wariness of mass marketing, a depressive self-questioning, an antifashion look—became very fashionable indeed.

Depending on one's point of view, it was either a great parade to lead or a massive load to drag. Kurt Cobain was not, by his nature, a parade leader.

While Nirvana toured Europe in the summer of 1991, U.S. buzz on the band had grown deafening. Weeks before *Nevermind*'s release, punk kids and industry insiders alike were talking about the album and swapping dubs of advance cassettes. Yet Kurt wasn't privy to much of this hype—or to the perks of stardom. In late July, he was evicted from his small Olympia apartment and sleeping in his car, an old Plymouth

ABOVE: By 1993, worldwide fame had taken a serious toll on Kurt's mental and physical well-being. Here, he is photographed on New Year's Day. Though he'd had a break from most public appearances, Kurt began the year depressed, with stomach pains and an increasingly serious drug addiction.

Valiant. More troubling though, Kurt had become a regular user of heroin (or "heroine," as he called it in his journal), a drug he had formerly eschewed but finally tried the previous fall, distraught over his breakup with Tobi Vail and seeking relief from his incessant stomach pains. By that summer, he was using the drug regularly; before Kurt had even become famous, he was succumbing to a popular rock-star temptation. Krist had warned him that heroin was more dangerous than other drugs he'd tried, but Kurt was confiding increasingly less in his loyal band mate.

The magnitude of Nirvana's burgeoning fame finally registered with Cobain in mid-September, on the eve of the album's release. At an in-store appearance in Seattle, the band was stunned when hundreds of fans showed up to an event expected to draw only a few dozen people. During the band's forty-five-minute live set in the shop, Kurt saw both of his ex-girlfriends, Vail and Marander, thrashing along, and he was flabbergasted when a pair of old schoolmates from Montesano approached him for autographs. Such public scenes only became more surreal as Nirvana kicked off a U.S. tour that fall. The band was booked for small venues, and in every city hundreds of fans were left without tickets, clamoring outside clubs from Detroit to New York.

The whirlwind of late 1991 brought about the pivotal change in Kurt's romantic life: the beginning of his relationship with Courtney Love. The couple had first met at a Nirvana gig in Portland, Oregon, in early

*ABOVE:* This photograph helps illustrate how Nirvana was able to draw such a diverse audience. Even in their physical appearance, the band successfully fused a punk aesthetic with classic rock-and-roll style: note Kurt's thick eyeliner, a popular fashion with goth rockers of the era like Nick Cave and the Cure, and, in contrast, Dave Grohl's baseball cap, which bears a famous Led Zeppelin logo.

1990, when he was still dating Tracy. He and Courtney flirted, and she corresponded with him later that year. But they didn't see each other again until a Los Angeles L7 show in the spring of 1991, as Nirvana and Courtney's band, Hole, were finishing their respective albums. Finally, after months of correspondence and talking about each other with mutual friends, in October Courtney found Kurt at a Nirvana show at the Metro in Chicago, and they officially began dating.

Within weeks, they were inseparable. Kurt felt a kinship with Courtney that he hadn't experienced in his previous relationships, and her influence was immediately apparent. Kurt's new girlfriend unquestionably encouraged his daring side. In November, Kurt scandalized the British press by describing, live on a U.K. television program, Courtney's sexual performance in terms generally considered too vulgar for television. While Courtney battled her own drug addiction and would occasionally indulge in heroin with him, her most profound influence was evident in his emergence as a rock star.

took the stage and—live on the air—strummed the first few chords of "Rape Me," panicking the MTV bigwigs into a cut-to-commercial frenzy before the band segued into "Lithium." Feeling triumphant, Kurt closed the performance by leading the band in trashing the set.

*ABOVE:* Nirvana performed at a New York City Tower Records store in late September 1991—a rare acoustic set. Kurt generally felt that in-store appearances should be accompanied by a performance, not just autograph signing, to make the appearance worthwhile for fans. Yet he was amazed by the throngs that would show up for these events.

*LEFT:* Nirvana played this Rock for Choice benefit in Seattle on October 25, 1991. Having become more political after his years in the Olympia rock scene, Kurt played a number of benefits during the band's short life span. His activism accelerated after meeting Courtney Love, who was involved in a number of progressive causes.

ABOVE: As Nirvana became video stars and *Nevermind* topped the charts, the band continued to be fiery in concert. They ended 1991 as the middle band on a three-act bill with Pearl Jam and the Red Hot Chili Peppers, and Nirvana was the inarguable star of the tour.

When Cobain wasn't courting controversy, it found him. By the time of the MTV awards, his personal life had changed dramatically—he was a husband, a father, and the focus of tabloid scrutiny. He and Love had married in February in Hawaii, and Courtney gave birth to Frances Bean Cobain in August. That same month, an interview the couple had given to *Vanity Fair* magazine came back to haunt them. The profile by Lynn Hirschberg, citing unnamed sources, intimated that not only Kurt but also Courtney had continued using heroin during the pregnancy. Within a week of Frances Bean's birth, the L.A. County Department of Children's Services, citing the *Vanity Fair* article, successfully petitioned to take the child out of the Cobains' care; the new parents were permitted to see her only in the company of a legally appointed guardian. Kurt, who had fallen instantly in love with his daughter and even had her first sonogram image reproduced on the sleeve of Nirvana's "Lithium" single, was devastated. Contrary to his nonconfrontational image, Kurt left furious, threatening messages on Hirschberg's answering machine, and he would do the same to other journalists he suspected of producing unflattering profiles.

ABOVE: This backstage scene was commonplace in 1990, as the band played a backbreaking itinerary of concerts in the United States and Europe.

If Cobain was wary of fame at his breakthrough, he came to despise it when his band was at the top. Between the *Vanity Fair* sideswipe and widespread speculation about his sobriety, Kurt felt persecuted and wanted to clarify himself to fans. A Nirvana singles-and-rarities disc released just before Christmas 1992, *Incesticide*, became notorious for its liner notes: Kurt's three-page essay articulating both the humbling rewards of rock stardom and his overwhelming discomfort with fame and the media microscope it brought. Recounting the perks he'd encountered on a recent U.K. trip, he expressed embarrassment at his good fortune, especially when meeting bands he loved that Nirvana was now outselling. He spewed anger that his wife, a "supreme example of dignity, ethics, and honesty," had been dragged through the mud. He cursed "music industry plankton"—the managers and media who wanted a piece of him. And he reserved special loathing for his dopiest frat-boy fans, the testosterone-fueled metalheads who'd alienated him as a youth— particularly a pair of teens who'd reportedly raped a girl while singing the lyrics to *Nevermind*'s "Polly." Never had a newly minted rock star sounded so alienated from his public, so uncomfortable with what a previous era's musicians would consider a dream life.

Yet Kurt's growing malaise also fueled his art, especially Nirvana's next album. A reaction against the press, the hype, and Kurt's own festering fears, *In Utero* would come to be known as Nirvana's angriest and most dissonant album. DGC Records, Nirvana's label, had concerns. The band brought in producer Steve Albini, formerly of punk band Big Black. With his indie-rock credentials and his insistence that a band should be "recorded," not produced, Albini had already brought out a raw, cacophonous sound in the Pixies, PJ Harvey, and the Jesus Lizard. Though Kurt had worked well with *Nevermind* producer Butch Vig, he felt that that album's radio-friendly signature—further sweetened by engineer Andy Wallace's punchy remix—had made the band sound "candy-ass," and he went out of his way to avoid repeating it.

Recorded in a swift two weeks in February 1993, *In Utero* featured some of Cobain's most jarring and direct punk songs, including "Milk It" and "Scentless Apprentice." But Kurt couldn't deny his gentler side or his pop sensibilities, which emerged on the sweet-and-sour "Heart-Shaped Box," the elegiac "Pennyroyal Tea," and the ironically pensive "Dumb." Indeed, both Cobain and his label underestimated the buried hooks on *In Utero*—Kurt had aimed to make an antipop record, and DGC battled with the band to withhold the "uncommercial" album from the market. Cobain finally agreed that Albini's sound was too stark and brought in Scott Litt, producer for R.E.M., to remix "Heart-Shaped Box" and "All Apologies" and make them more accessible.

The album would have been more forbidding had Cobain been permitted to release it under his original title, *I Hate Myself and Want to Die*. It was a sentiment Kurt expressed, in both his words and his demeanor, continually in the final year of his life. Though Kurt and Courtney finally regained custody of their daughter in the spring of 1993, their relationship grew more tempestuous, with recurring fights over Kurt's drug benders

*ABOVE:* It's appropriate that this photo was taken in England, at the moment Nirvana broke—it closely resembles a famous photo of the young Beatles looking down a stairwell, taken at the start of their career in England. The only difference is in the two bands' facial expressions. In contrast to the four smiling Beatles, Nirvana's members were already growing mistrustful of their newfound celebrity.

and his insistence on keeping guns in the house. On several occasions, police came to the Cobain house on domestic disturbance calls; in at least one incident, Kurt had locked himself in the bathroom and threatened to kill himself. His stomach problems persisted and, despite the access he and Courtney had to top-notch medical care, seemed to resist diagnosis by an array of physicians. No pain treatment worked as well for Kurt as heroin, which lurked in the background of his daily life and colored all of his interactions. Courtney saved him from overdosing on several occasions, and by the middle of 1993, reviving him had become routine. At this point, his personal relationships had deteriorated considerably: he'd grown alienated from his wife, ceased speaking to his band mates, and estranged all of his friends, save those who shared his addiction.

Looking back on Cobain's final months, it's a wonder that so much art shone through the chaos. Released in September 1993, *In Utero* was hailed by many critics as a tour de force; others, wary of Kurt's antipop smugness, proclaimed the album too self-conscious, but it topped the charts in its first week. Supporting the album was the fever-dream video for "Heart-Shaped Box," perhaps the purest depiction of Kurt's fascinations: deformed dolls, fetuses hanging from trees, and Christ figures—one strapped into a hospital bed—all made appearances. Shocking and inspired though the video was, ironically, it stood out less on the MTV of 1993 than "Teen Spirit" had two years earlier. The channel had adapted its content and tone to suit the times—a shift Nirvana had precipitated.

LEFT: Kurt visits Hilverstrum Studios for a Holland radio show on November 25, 1991. Nirvana had also recorded radio shows earlier that fall for legendary U.K. deejay John Peel. The band was now accustomed to fancier recording facilities after having made *Nevermind* in Los Angeles' well-equipped Sound City studios. Needless to say, Nirvana's record-making experiences in 1991 were a far cry from its raw 1988–89 sessions with Jack Endino in a tiny Seattle studio.

BELOW: *Nevermind* went gold—half a million copies sold—within weeks of its release in the fall of 1991. DGC Records, Nirvana's label, had initially hoped to sell one-fifth of that.

Nirvana produced an awesome cacophony for a threesome—it was among the greatest power trios rock has ever known.

A very successful European tour with Sonic Youth in August 1991 culminated in a show at England's Reading Festival that won rave notices. The band invited Eugene Kelly of the Vaselines—one of Kurt's favorite bands—onstage to perform "Molly's Lips," a Vaselines' original that Nirvana recorded live and released as a single that year. Also present at the festival was Courtney Love, with boyfriend Billy Corgan, of the Smashing Pumpkins, in tow. Kurt later recalled that year's festival as one of the greatest moments of his life.

*RIGHT AND BELOW:* Here, Kurt fronts Nirvana at a Halloween 1991 show in Seattle. Kurt and Krist (below) hang out backstage after their Halloween performance. Sales of *Nevermind* were fast approaching platinum status (1 million copies sold). The Santa hats were rather prophetic—Nirvana would be the hit band of Christmas 1991. Or at least it would be considered the post-Christmas hit: thousands of kids returned the CDs their parents got them that year and exchanged them for *Nevermind*. The album would go on to sell 10 million copies.

*OPPOSITE:* Nirvana returned to England in November 1991, three months after their triumphant Reading Festival appearance, to kick off a European tour to support *Nevermind*. By now the album was released and climbing charts on both sides of the Atlantic

Nirvana first played NBC-TV's *Saturday Night Live* on January 11, 1992, the headiest of heady times for the band. Just the week before, *Billboard* magazine revealed that *Nevermind* was the #1 album in America, and the *SNL* showcase was Nirvana's largest live television audience to date. The band's managers were just becoming aware of Kurt's growing drug problem. Sporting a bad dye job that left his hair strawberry-red, Kurt delivered a tense, wobbly performance of "Smells Like Teen Spirit," now confirmed as both a generational anthem and a pop hit. Later, they performed a potent "Territorial Pissings" against the wishes of the show's producers that ended with a trademark destruction of instruments. At the close of the show, when the band and guest host Rob Morrow came onstage to say goodnight, Kurt and Krist kissed live on the air, a spontaneous act by Krist that Kurt later claimed was staged.

**OPPOSITE AND LEFT:** Nirvana picked up two awards at the 1992 MTV Video Music Awards show: Best New Artist and Best Alternative Video. The band sent a Michael Jackson impersonator to pick up the latter award. On the show's back lot, Kurt and Courtney were confronted by a belligerent Axl Rose and his girlfriend, Stephanie Seymour; no punches were thrown, but Kurt's wit and Courtney's sarcasm made the metal god and his model girlfriend look fatuous and embarrasingly passé.

**ABOVE:** The awards show served as a coming-out party for month-old Frances Bean, who was permitted to be with her parents only in the presence of a court-appointed guardian.

*ABOVE:* By the middle of 1992, rumors had spread so widely of Cobain's destructive habits and concert no-shows that Kurt responded—in his inimitable, uncanny fashion. That August, Nirvana headlined England's Reading Festival, and Kurt went onstage in a wheelchair and medical smock, slumped over, seemingly strung out and wasted. Just as the audience was beginning to believe that the rumors were true, he leaped out of the chair, guitar in hand, and ripped into *Nevermind*'s pulverizing "Breed," exhilarating the crowd.

*OPPOSITE:* Kurt practically programmed that year's festival: his favorite bands, including the Melvins, the Screaming Trees, L7, and Eugenius, were on the lineup. Despite the growing chorus of rumors that Cobain's addictions were overwhelming him and causing his erratic behavior, Nirvana performed a blistering 25-song set spanning the group's career.

**ABOVE:** Now widely perceived as the voice of his generation, Kurt wrote and recorded *In Utero*, his first post-fame album, with a heavy burden of expectation hanging over the band. Fortunately, he had already drafted early versions of some of the album's strongest songs two to three years earlier. By the time Nirvana regrouped to record in 1993, Kurt came equipped with some of his most sardonic songs.

**LEFT:** In late 1992, with publicity for *Nevermind* winding down and the band exhausted, Kurt pulled away from the spotlight for several months. His only contact with the public that winter was in his vituperative liner notes to the early-recordings collection *Incesticide*.

**OPPOSITE:** Kurt and Courtney kill time during the recording of *In Utero*. There was actually little downtime—thanks to the bare-bones recording style of producer Steve Albini, the bulk of the album was laid down in only two weeks in February 1993.

OPPOSITE: Kurt and Courtney married in Hawaii when she was already three months pregnant. Worried that their drug use would affect the baby, they visited a series of doctors and were relieved to learn their unborn child was gestating normally. Love cleaned herself up, endured months of withdrawal on top of the discomfort of pregnancy, and, on August 18, 1992 in Los Angeles, gave birth to a healthy girl, Frances Bean Cobain.

ABOVE: With the release of In Utero, Nirvana embarked on their first major arena tour. Despite Kurt's petulance onstage, the tour drew solid reviews.

RIGHT: Wearing a dress was one of Kurt's favorite subversive onstage acts—a surefire way to antagonize the type-A male fans Nirvana had unwittingly acquired in its rise to stardom.

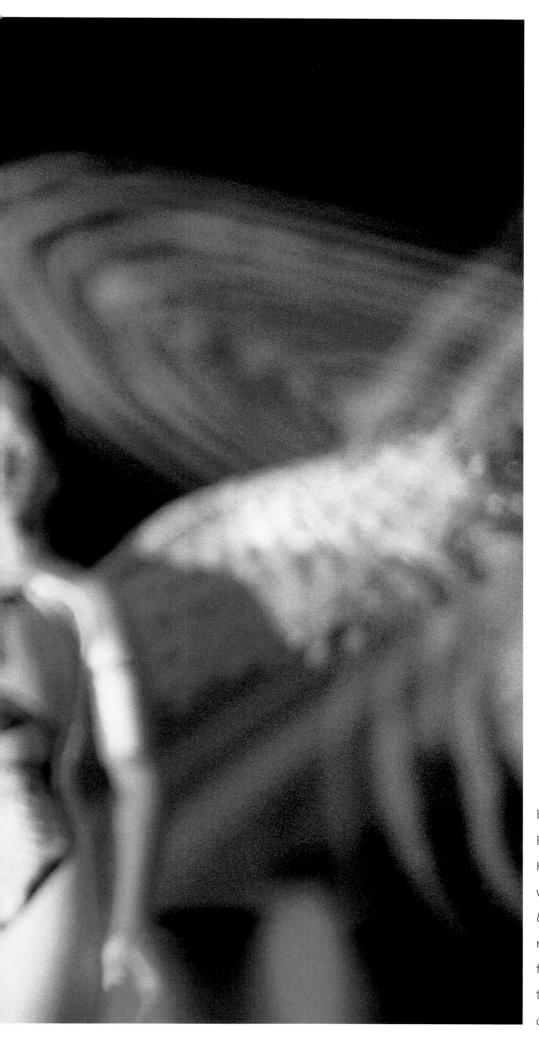

Evident in the lyrics for "Heart-Shaped Box," and in Nirvana's music videos, Kurt's fascination with the female body was a major thematic thread on *In Utero*. The album's cover featured the now-famous medical model of the female anatomy, which was constructed to life-size proportions as a stage prop on the band's 1993 tour.

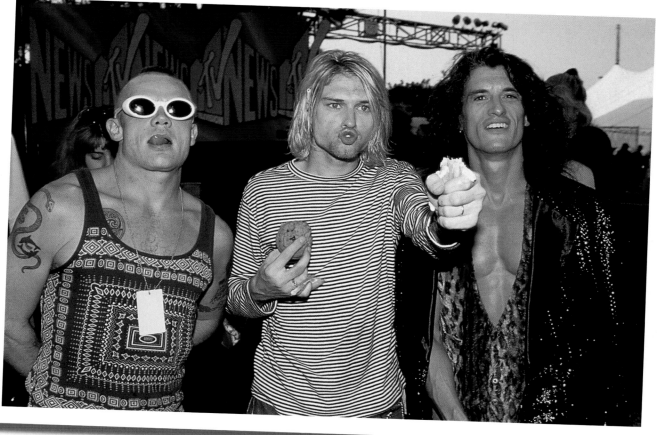

*OPPOSITE:* Kurt posed dutifully for pictures with rock royalty at the 1993 MTV awards, including Flea of the Red Hot Chili Peppers (bottom, left), Joe Perry of Aerosmith (bottom, right), and Peter Gabriel (top, right).

*LEFT AND BELOW:* Though Nirvana wasn't the night's big winner—Pearl Jam took home the most statues—Kurt and Courtney presided over the MTV back lot like royalty, with Frances Bean in tow. Amid the backstage glitz, Kurt seemed happiest cavorting with his daughter.

*OPPOSITE:* Despite being one of the world's biggest rock stars, in the last year of his life Kurt hardly bothered with maintaining the grunge image, eschewing even the flannel shirts he helped to popularize. The big sunglasses he wore were his only rock-star accoutrement, probably worn more to block out the world than to look cool.

*ABOVE:* Though never officially credited as such, guitarist Pat Smear (right), a friend of Kurt's and Dave Grohl's, was effectively the fourth member of Nirvana in its final months. He first performed with the band in their final *Saturday Night Live* appearance on September 25, 1993, and toured with them in subsequent months. Formerly of seminal punk band the Germs, Smear had already endured one junkie bandmate—Germs singer Darby Crash, who died of an overdose in 1980—so there was little the drug-abusing Kurt could do to phase him.

ABOVE: The second week of November '93 found the *In Utero* tour in New York City. Nirvana played two shows that week, at the New York Coliseum and Roseland Ballroom, but spent much of their time at the SST Rehearsal Studio in New Jersey preparing for MTV *Unplugged*, now considered one of the most significant performances of their career.

OPPOSITE: Backstage at a Seattle concert near the holidays, Kurt ignored the photographers who'd come to shoot his picture on assignment and instead let his hometown friend Alice Wheeler take several spontaneous pictures of him, Frances Bean, and a haphazardly placed Christmas garland.

Kurt Cobain in Seattle  Dec. 13, 93                    Photo by Alice Wheeler

ABOVE: A picture from Kurt's final promotional photo session, less than a year before his death.

LEFT: Photographed in December 1993 as the *In Utero* tour prepared to enter Europe, Kurt is barely able to conceal his exhaustion and weariness. He felt strung out, alone, and emotionally divorced from family, band mates, and friends.

BELOW: After going missing for almost a week, Kurt Cobain was finally found on April 8, 1994. An electrician installing a security system found his body in the greenhouse atop his garage. Authorities ruled the case a suicide and said that Cobain had been dead for three days.

OPPOSITE: It would be nearly a decade before Nirvana fans would hear Kurt's last recorded song. "You Know You're Right" was the only Cobain composition that the band completed in a brief January 1994 recording session; the bulk of the other songs were Grohl compositions that were later rerecorded by his band the Foo Fighters. Released in the fall of 2002, "You Know You're Right" topped the modern rock charts, a fitting coda to the decade-long dominance of the Nirvana sound on rock radio.

RIGHT: "We remember Kurt for what he was: caring, generous, and sweet," Krist Novoselic told fans in his taped message at the Seattle vigil. "Let's keep the music with us. We'll always have it, forever."

BELOW: In her taped message to fans, Courtney read aloud portions of Kurt's suicide note and incited the crowd to yell out their anger at Kurt for taking his life. "I'm really sorry, and I feel the same way you do," she said, choking back tears. "I don't know what I could have done."

# ALL IN ALL

W HAT COBAIN'S FRIENDS, FAMILY, AND FANS SHARE IS A FEELING of waste at Kurt's loss and a sense that an extraordinary voice has been silenced. Despite his achievements, it's difficult to argue that Kurt lived a full life or even a rich one. So much of his accomplishment was paired inextricably with sadness and pain, and he barely enjoyed any of his success, giving himself neither the time nor the will. He was hardly unappreciated; perhaps Kurt was loved too well by people he had no intention of reaching—peers he had no idea shared his feelings of alienation, self-doubt, and defiance. Though his death was commemorated by pages of instant eulogies, the thousands who gathered in Seattle in the days after his death were a more eloquent testament. They were a proxy for the millions who felt that Kurt spoke for them.

Nearly a decade later, Cobain's spirit continues to haunt the creative arts, for better and for worse—from the cadre of postgrunge quiet-loud bands that clog modern rock radio to the postmodern, self-conscious sarcasm that pop culture has never quite gotten over. It's a testament to Cobain's singular talent that no artist has recaptured Nirvana's blend of droll irony, unabashed emotion, and raw power. When "You Know You're Right" returned Nirvana to the radio in late 2002, the howl of Kurt's voice from the afterlife was like a corrective to fans who'd waited years to hear the real thing. Instantly familiar, the song reunited a generation with a voice that for them had become primal.

Kurt Cobain's legacy remains not just in his indelible songs but in the spirit of subversion he incited, the misfit voices he amplified until they were loud enough to be heard worldwide. To this day, it amazes us, the will of instinct.

This beloved picture of Kurt—emblazoned on thousands of T-shirts and magazine covers since his death—captures the artist as most fans remember him. His tousled hair, eyeliner, and goatee recall an alt-rock icon.

ABOVE: Kurt performs on the *In Utero* tour, with the angel–medical model stage prop directly behind him. This image, taken about a half-year before Kurt's death, now comes burdened with symbolism and irony.

OPPOSITE: Defying all attempts to save it, Kurt's extraordinary life seemed to glow briefly, radiantly, and then extinguish itself. All but certain to burn out, he was never in danger of fading away.

# INDEX

# PHOTO CREDITS

©Alice Wheeler: 21 top, 21 bottom, 23, 27, 29 all, 31, 33 top, 33 bottom, 38, 41 top, 44-45, 52 bottom, 85 top, 85 bottom, 87 top, 89 top

Angles: ©**Ed Esposito**: 5, 20, 54

AP Wide World: 26 bottom

©Edie Baskin Studios: 68-69

©Jay Blakesberg: 10, 37 top, 77 top, 82, 93

©Jim Blanchard: 25, 30 right

©Anna Maria Di Santo: 77 bottom

Corbis: 43, 51, 62-63, 78-79, 91; ©**Karen Mason Bair**: 66; ©**Lee Celano**: 70; ©**Joe Giron**: 67; ©**John Van Hasselt**: 87 bottom; ©**Howard Jacqueline**: 50, 61; ©**Tim Owen**: 55; ©**Ian Titlon**: 42 bottom

©Justin Hampton: 37 top right

©Jones Photo Company: 13

Courtesy of Leland Cobain: 12, 14, 15, 16, 18, 19, 26 top, 40 bottom

London Features International: 80 top right; ©**Andrew Catlin**: 24 top; ©**Frank Forcino**: 84; ©**Mike Hashimoto**: 58 top; ©**Kevin Mazur**: 71, 80 bottom, 81 top, 92

Courtesy of Montesano Junior-Senior High School (1980 Sylvan—yearbook): 17

©Raymond Pettibon: 33 bottom right

Redferns: 84; ©**Paul Bergen**: 41 bottom

Retna: ©**Jeff Davy**: 65 top; ©**Steve Double**: 74 bottom; ©**Steve Granitz**: 81 bottom; ©**Charles Hoselton**: 11, 86, 88, 89 bottom; ©**Yori Lenguette**: 83; ©**Michel Linssen**: 59 top, 74 top; ©**Tony Mottram**: 56; ©**Charles Peterson**: 24 bottom, 34-35, 40 top, 49, 52 top, 73, 75; ©**Steve Pyke**: 60; ©**Soren Rud**: 59 bottom; ©**Ed Sirrs**: 65; ©**Stephen Sweet**: 76; ©**Kelly Swift**: 80 top left; ©**Chris Taylor**: 72; ©**Niels Van Iperen**: 1, 6, 64

Star File: 54 top

©Ian Tilton, www.iantilton.com: 2, 30, 32, 36 all, 37 bottom, 39, 43 top, 46

©Kirk Weddle: 9